EXPLORE YOUR WORLD

PHYSICAL SCIENCE

Big Machines

CARLOTA CRUZ

TABLE OF CONTENTS

What Are Big Machines?.................................. 2
Machines that Build Buildings....................... 4
Machines in the Water.................................. 10
Machines in the Air 14
Glossary/Index 20

PIONEER VALLEY EDUCATIONAL PRESS, INC

WHAT ARE BIG MACHINES?

Big machines are large powerful **vehicles** that help us do big jobs. Big machines are used to **transport** heavy objects from one place to another. They also are used to knock things down. Big machines are used on the land, in the air, and in the water.

3

MACHINES THAT
BUILD BUILDINGS

Bulldozers are large machines that ride on tracks to give them **traction** to move along uneven roads. They have a **blade** that is used to push things or dig into the ground. Bulldozers help get the ground ready for building new houses or office buildings.

tracks

▶▶▶ **When the blade pushes down, it cuts into the ground. When it pushes forward, it moves the dirt.**

blade

Diggers, or excavators,
are big machines used
to dig large holes in the ground.
The excavator has a long arm
called a boom that moves up and down.
At the end of the arm is a bucket
with teeth that is used
to break hard ground or rocks.

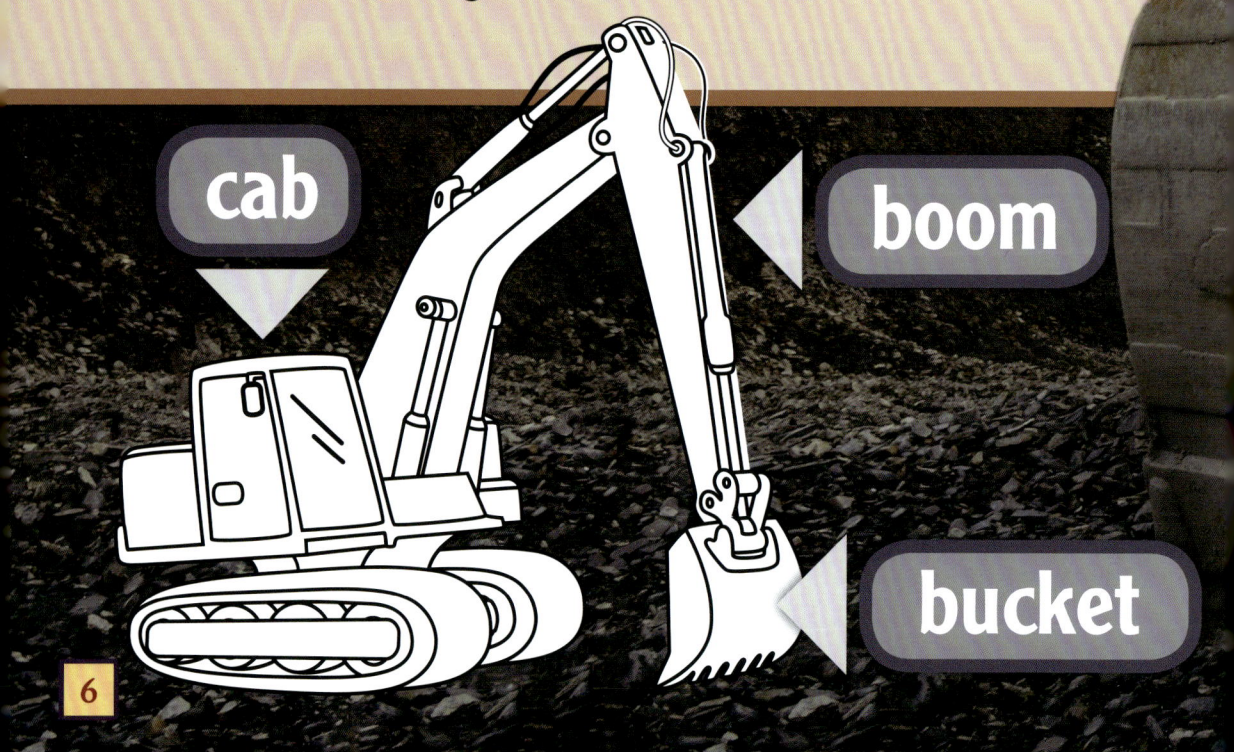

cab

boom

bucket

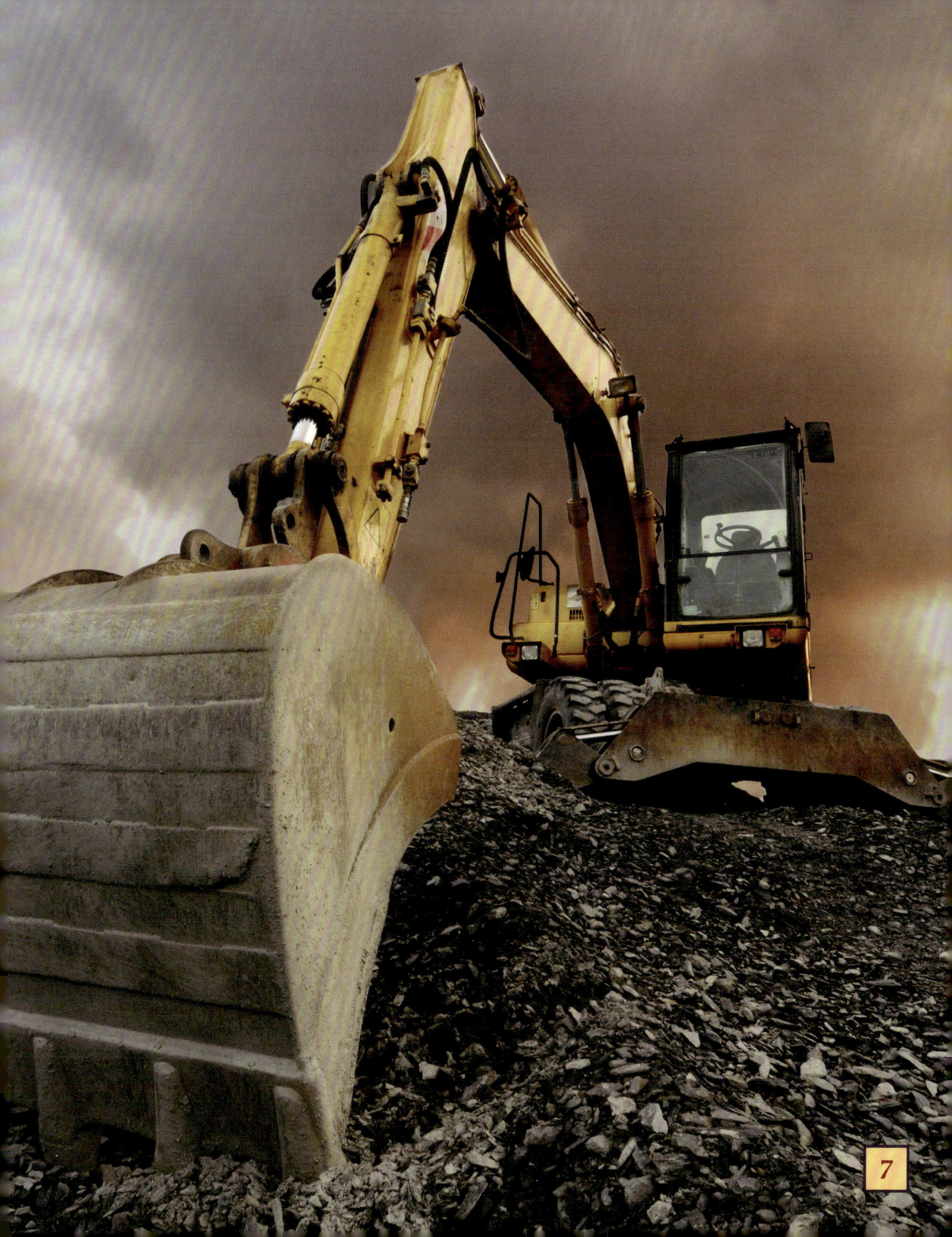

Cranes are big machines often used to help build tall buildings because they can **hoist** or lift things. A crane can hoist very heavy loads. It can be used to move big things from side to side and up and down.

Cranes are used to help unload heavy boxes off of cargo ships.

This crane has a big ball on it. The crane is being used to **DISMANTLE** an old building. The crane swings the ball into the building's wall to knock it down.

MORE TO EXPLORE

9

MACHINES IN THE WATER

Many machines are used in the water. They are used to carry heavy loads or to move things.

Tugboats are small but powerful machines used to help move big boats, ships, and **barges**. They push, or sometimes tow, the ships in places that are small or crowded, like a **harbor**.

Some tugboats help when there is a fire at sea.

11

An aircraft carrier is a very large ship that carries planes and helicopters. The aircraft carrier has a large **deck** that is used as an airplane runway. Planes can take off and land on an aircraft carrier.

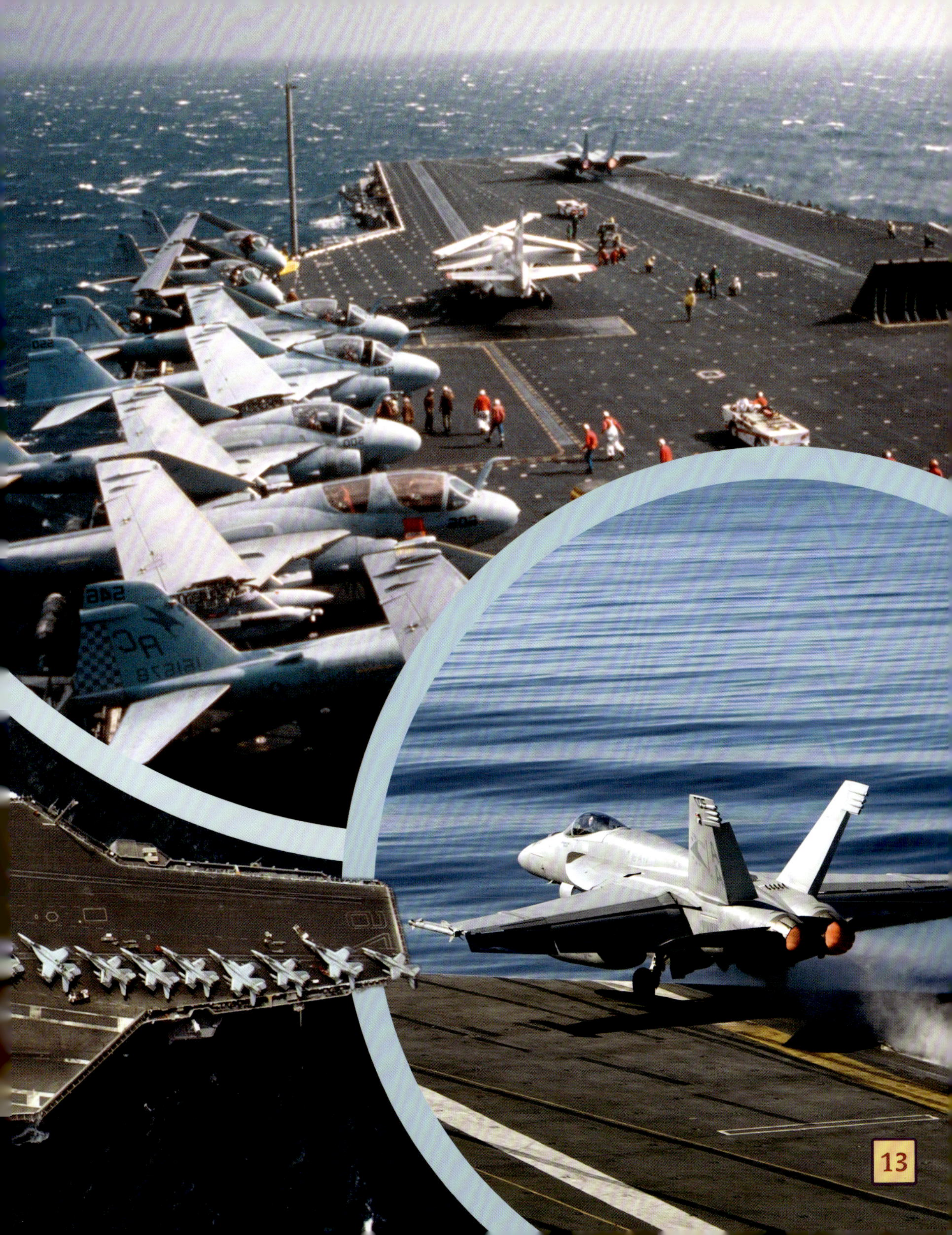

MACHINES IN THE AIR

Machines are used in the air.
They are used to move and carry things.

Airplanes are flying machines.
These vehicles carry people
and things to many places.

Some airplanes are very small
and are built to carry
only one or two people.

The Wright brothers built the first airplane.

Some airplanes carry packages and mail.

Some airplanes carry many people from one place to another.

Helicopters are used for many things. They are used to rescue people who are hurt, carrying them to a safe place.

Some helicopters help fight fires.

Some helicopters have **cables** and hooks for carrying heavy loads from one place to another.

The space station
is a huge machine in space.
It is about as big as a football field
and flies high above the earth.
It has places for people
to live and work.
It carries people and **equipment**
that help us learn more about space.

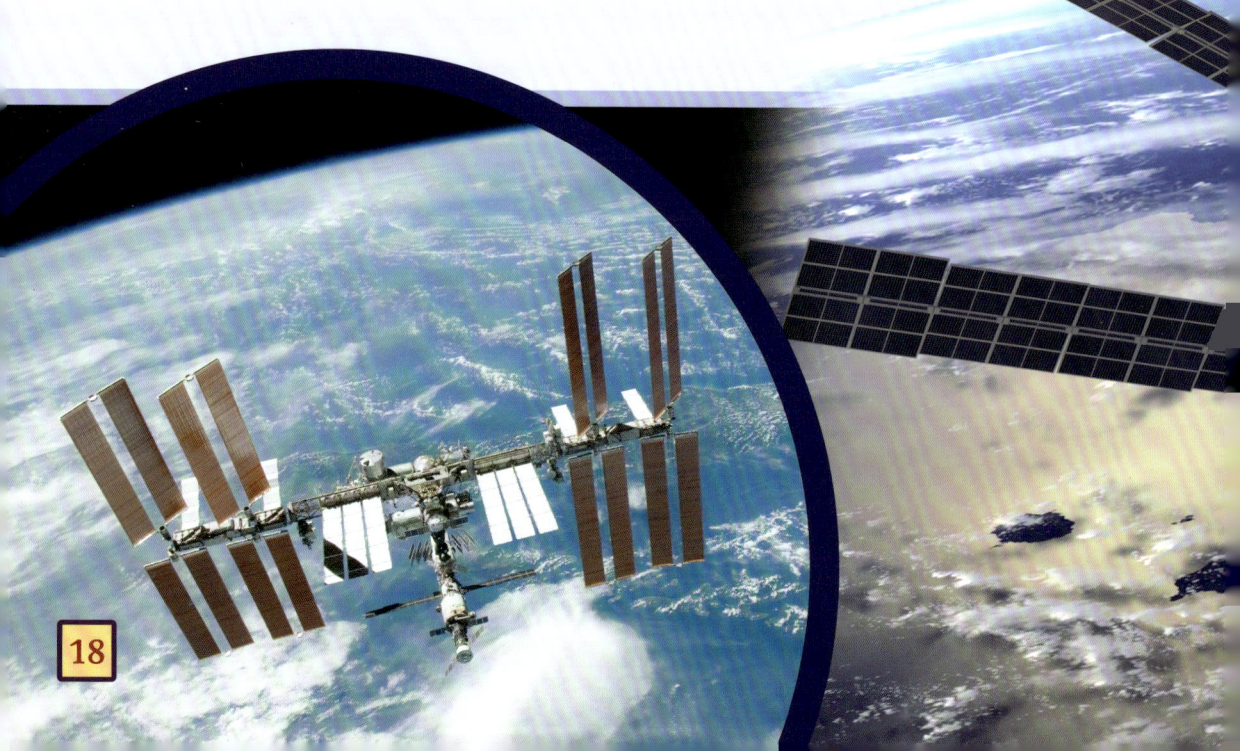

19

helicopter

pile driver

space station

tugboat

barge

What is your **favorite** **big** machine?

GLOSSARY

barges
flat-bottomed boats that carry goods on rivers and canals

blade
the cutting part of a tool, used for scraping and digging

cables
very strong thick ropes, wires, or chains

deck
a flat surface with no roof

dismantle
knock down

equipment
tools needed for special work

harbor
water near land that is deep enough for ships to sail in

hoist
to lift up

traction
the force that causes a moving object to stick against the surface it is moving along

transport
to carry from one place to another

vehicles
machines used to carry people from one place to another

INDEX

air craft carrier 12-13
airplanes 14-15
barges 10-11
blade 4-5
boom 6-7
break 6
bulldozers 4-5
cables 17
cargo ships 8
carry 10, 15, 17
cranes 8-9
deck 12-13
dig 4-5, 6-7
digger 6-7
equipment 18
excavator 6-7
harbor 10-11
helicopters 12, 16-17
hoist 8
knock down 2, 9
push 4-5, 10
rescue 16
space station 18-19
tow 10-11
tracks 4
tugboats 10-11
vehicles 2, 14

20